The Cotswolds Year Round Walks

Spring, Summer, **Autumn** & Winter

John & Angela Cooper

COUNTRYSIDE BOOKS
NEWBURY BERKSHIRE

First published 2021
© 2021 John & Angela Cooper

COUNTRYSIDE BOOKS
3 Catherine Road
Newbury, Berkshire

To view our complete range of books,
please visit us at
www.countrysidebooks.co.uk

ISBN 978 1 84674 401 3

'For Emmy'

Produced by The Letterworks Ltd., Reading
Typeset by KT Designs, St Helens
Printed in Poland

Introduction

Walks are wonderful at any time of the year, but some really shine in certain seasons. The stark beauty of bare trees silhouetted against the sky in winter; open landscapes in summer; the startling clarity of a blue sky in spring contrasting with the green and white tones of emerging life; autumnal colours showcased in woodlands.

The geology of the Cotswolds, quite literally its bedrock, determines the distinct character and appearance of the different regions. This is not only evident in the general appearance and topography of an area, it can also be seen in the villages and its buildings. In the northern parts, honey hues bring warmth to winter walks, while the creamier and greyer stone as you travel south offers a welcome coolness in summer.

Whilst walks have been chosen to complement particular seasons, there is a pleasure in re-treading the same walk throughout the year, comparing the different elements – the verdant field of summer crops becomes the barren, ploughed and almost alien expanse of winter. The spring woodland, rich in the colour and sounds of new life, evolves beyond summer into the dying world of autumn with its falling leaves and a chill in the air. Watching hares 'box', or a herd of silent deer outlined against a bare backdrop allows us to experience seasonal change and the wonder of nature first hand. The combination of the visual and the sounds, smells and feel of the countryside provides a sense of well-being.

This collection of walks gives just a taste of the beauty and variety of the Cotswolds, far from the more familiar areas frequented by visitors. Those walkers who love geology, scenery and nature will also value the rich history of the region and the puzzles and questions that lead to new learning – how to recognise a forgotten stretch of a Roman road, a ture (walled routes to drive animals to watering holes) or a dewpond. Walking along a ture on a cold winter's morning provides a reminder of the harshness of medieval life. A now moss-covered Roman road, with buds emerging in the hedgerows and the sound of spring lambs bleating in the distance, briefly transports you back to the world of marching legionaries. An ancient holloway, or sunken lane, with deep banks and overhanging ferns can, just for a moment, give a sense of life in a remote medieval settlement. Walking through nature stimulates the imagination, a welcome break from the technology-driven modern world.

The Cotswolds Year Round Walks

Seasonal walks provide an opportunity to connect with nature on a physical, emotional and mental level. Whenever you travel these often remote and forgotten paths, you preserve and maintain invaluable rights of way for future generations.

We have tried to be as accurate as possible with directions, balancing giving too much with too little information. If routes or signs are unclear, maps and compasses are always useful when in doubt.

Whether you explore the heights of Uley Bury or the enclosed secret world of Edgeworth, the wide-open spaces of Aldsworth or the tranquil beauty of the water meadows near Sherborne, we hope you enjoy these special places. Whichever season you walk in, and whichever walk you choose, happy walking.

John & Angela Cooper

Publisher's Note

We hope that you obtain considerable enjoyment from this book; great care has been taken in its preparation. Although at the time of publication all routes followed public rights of way or permitted paths, diversion orders can be made and permissions withdrawn.

We cannot, of course, be held responsible for such diversion orders or any inaccuracies in the text which result from these or any other changes to the routes, nor any damage which might result from walkers trespassing on private property. We are anxious, though, that all the details covering the walks are kept up to date, and would therefore welcome information from readers which would be relevant to future editions.

The simple sketch maps that accompany the walks in this book are based on notes made by the author whilst surveying the routes on the ground. They are designed to show you how to reach the start and to point out the main features of the overall circuit, and they contain a progression of numbers that relate to the paragraphs of the text.

However, for the benefit of a proper map, we do recommend that you purchase the relevant Ordnance Survey sheet covering your walk. Ordnance Survey maps are widely available, especially through booksellers and local newsagents.

The River Windrush

1 Sherborne & Water Meadows
Water, weirs and wildlife

4¼ miles (7 km)

WALK HIGHLIGHTS

In contrast to Aldsworth some 3 miles away (walk 10) with its high and open terrain, this area on the opposite side of the A40 generally passes through sheltered valleys with streams meandering along at a gentle pace. From the car park there are a number of walking options, although this one takes in the lovely atmosphere of the water meadows, the River Windrush and the weirs and watermills along the way. Spring showcases the amount and variety of birds and wild flowers on the walk, and the first part, taking in parkland with old established trees in bud, provides a welcome reminder of the warm months ahead. The water meadows have sluice gates that control the flow of water into the meadows. This provides a rich and fertile environment for a diverse collection of birds, animals and plants. Otters live here, albeit more secretive inhabitants. Herons, corn buntings and yellowhammers are often seen, along with red kites. In late spring and summer, dragonflies are a common sight. The distinctive 'plop' sound of water voles as they enter the water can sometimes be heard. Just past the bridge at stage 1 look out for boulders and stones lying

5

The Cotswolds Year Round Walks

STARTING POINT & PARKING: Water Meadows Car Park at Northfield Barn (NT). **Sat Nav:** GL54 3DL.

MAP: OS Explorer OL 45 The Cotswolds. **Grid Ref:** SP 175154.
  what3words: litigate.grafted.afflict

TERRAIN: Field edges, country tracks and paths. Some quiet country roads. Gentle gradients.

FOOD & DRINK: The Fox Inn, Great Barrington, Burford, OX18 4TB. ☎ 01451 844385. This riverside inn and restaurant serves traditional British pub fare made with local and seasonal ingredients. There is also a daily specials board.
The Inn for All Seasons, Burford, OX18 4TN. ☎ 01451 844324. An attractive 16th-century inn with plenty of pub favourites on the menu, but you'd be wise to book ahead if you're wanting food.

abandoned, faint echoes of a once busy, and now long absent, watermill. This was Dodd's Mill, an early corn mill mentioned in the *Domesday Book* but abandoned by the early 20th century. Just beyond a weir is the River Windrush. Pausing on the bridge and looking at Windrush Mill provides what must be one of the most beautiful of Cotswold scenes.

THE WALK

1 **[SP 175154]** From the car park return to the road and turn right. Walk downhill for about 100 metres and then turn left onto the **Sabrina Way**. Follow the Sabrina Way through a wood, down into the water meadows and along to the river, crossing a footbridge and then, leaving the Sabrina Way, stay with the footpath and pass the remains of **Dodd's Mill**.

2 **[SP 189152]** Pass by the remains of the mill and follow the path as it sweeps around to the left and uphill. When the path meets a track go right and follow this track for about ½ mile before passing the imposing Grade II listed **Manor Farm**. Continue past the farm by the left-hand edge of a field and, at the corner, turn right and gently descend towards a copse. As the path emerges from the copse turn left and walk through two fields and then turn right through a gate and through a scrubby field towards the river.

spring

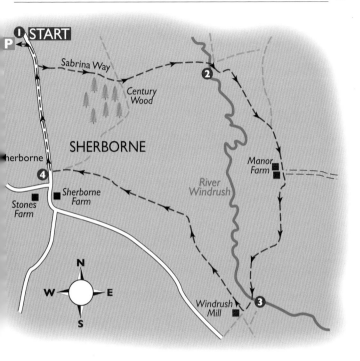

[SP 192135] Cross the **River Windrush** by the footbridge near **Windrush Mill**. Follow the path uphill to a lane and immediately turn right into a field and right again onto the footpath which initially runs parallel with the river. The footpath crosses through several fields to return towards **Sherborne**.

[SP 177146] In just over a mile you will emerge onto the Sherborne to Clapton road, where you turn right and pass over the bridge. Walk uphill to return to the **Water Meadows car park**.

spring

Rough Bank

2 The Camp
Up hill and down dale

2½ miles (4 km)

WALK HIGHLIGHTS

It is unclear how The Camp got its name. Possibly it is related to Neolithic camps (there are Neolithic burial chambers near the village) or it could have been a Civil War encampment. Whatever its origins, the entire walk is a naturalist's delight. Rough Bank Reserve is a cornucopia of rare plants and wildlife. It is a prime example of old flowery pasture, with lime-loving plants, including many varieties of spring flowering orchids. There are a remarkable 550 species of moth, and more than 30 different types of butterfly. In spring the beech woods at Famish Hill are full of birdsong and the distinctive drumming sound of woodpeckers, while

8

STARTING POINT & PARKING: Rough Bank Reserve car park. Approaching from the north, continue through The Camp and along Calf Way, past a left-hand fork just outside The Camp, the reserve entrance is about 170 metres further along on the right. **Sat Nav:** GL6 7HN.

MAP: OS Explorer 179 Gloucester, Cheltenham & Stroud. **Grid Ref:** SO 914087. **what3words:** defected.gears.lazy

TERRAIN: Footpaths through fields and some forest track. Steep in places. Some parts muddy after rain.

FOOD & DRINK: Foston's Ash Inn, The Camp, Stroud, GL6 7ES. ☎ 01452 863262. This award-winning inn has a lovely beer garden and children's play area, as well as welcoming indoor dining. The seasonal menu consists of free-range and locally sourced ingredients.

catkins hang thickly over the banks. Deer can sometimes be seen close at hand before they silently and swiftly retreat up hillsides. Be prepared for steep hills and equally deep valleys, this is an invigorating walk.

THE WALK

[SO 912086] From the parking area, walk down the track to the hedge which leads away to the right and turn right to follow this. Follow the footpath through two kissing gates and then through a field. The path then runs down through stables.

[SO 911092] At the end of the stables cross over the stile onto a track and turn left down through **Famish Hill**. Follow this all the way down to the end of the woodland. Keep to the footpath as it leads straight on through a gate, ignoring the tracks to the left and to the right. As the path continues to descend into a steep valley follow the contour around to **Dillay Farm**.

[SO 899087] Just before a gate at **Dillay Farm** turn left and descend the steep slope to the footbridge in the valley floor. Cross the footbridge and turn half-right and walk towards a stile marked by a tall white post.

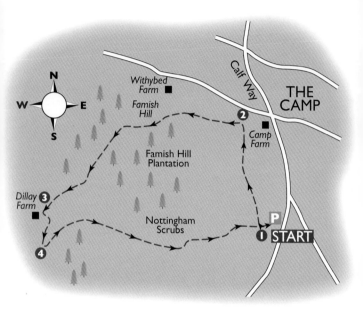

4 **[SO 898085]** Cross over the stile and after 10 metres turn left uphill. After about 200 metres there is a fork, take the right-hand path which leads past **Beech Cottage**. Follow the path as it passes through the woods and gradually uphill through **Nottingham Scrubs** to return through a metal gate to the **Rough Bank car park**. Just after the gate is another gate on the left leading to the **Rough Bank meadow** which is well worth a visit.

spring

View from Uley Bury

3 Uley Bury
Flying high

4 miles (6.3 km)

WALK HIGHLIGHTS

The initial ascent up Cam Peak is challenging but worth it for the sweeping views across to the River Severn from the top. Uley Bury is an impressive Iron Age hillfort overlooking the Severn Vale. The hill itself is a spur of the Cotswold escarpment, part of it a Site of Special Scientific Interest with an impressive mix of fossils such as ammonites. A combination of Jurassic limestone and unspoilt grassland makes this an important area for wildlife. Birds including kestrels and yellowhammers can be seen flying overhead. On three sides the steep natural slopes of the hill provide a panoramic outlook. Following the fort's rampart around, the Tyndale Monument becomes visible on the horizon, and the eagle-eyed might spot the Sugar Loaf by Abergavenny, and May Hill near Ross-on-Wye. In spring, bluebells cover the floor of the woods while primroses, daffodils

11

The Cotswolds Year Round Walks

STARTING POINT & PARKING: Cam Peak Car Park. **Sat Nav:** GL11 5HJ.

MAP: OS Explorer 167 Thornbury, Dursley & Yate. **Grid Ref:** ST 767993. **what3words:** shackles.elects.cycles

TERRAIN: Hilly tracks, with gradients of a moderate to challenging nature, wooded in places, and some very quiet lanes.

FOOD & DRINK: The Old Crown Inn, 17 The Green, Uley, Dursley, GL11 5SN. ☎ 01453 860502. This 17th-century coaching inn offers a traditional menu and locally brewed ales are served at the bar along with a wide range of drinks.

and violets grow on the banks bordering the paths. Parts of the route can be muddy and at times steep, especially leaving Uley Bury, but this is a small price to pay for what the walk has to offer.

THE WALK

1 **[ST 767993]** From the car park turn towards the distinctive **Cam Peak** and follow the footpath which runs to the left of the house on the hillside. Alternatively follow the trail right up the peak which might be easier underfoot in muddy conditions and will afford magnificent views over the **Severn Estuary**.

2 **[ST 769992]** As the slope eases the path meets up with the **Cotswold Way**. Turn left and follow the Cotswold Way up the hill and along the summit of **Cam Long Down** and then as it descends through fields towards some farm buildings where it emerges onto a lane. Again follow the sign-posted Cotswold Way as it passes some farms and uphill towards the northern apex of the **Uley Bury hillfort**.

3 **[ST 786993]** On reaching the road by the **Coaley Wood** lay-by turn right into the **Uley Bury hillfort** and at the entrance turn left by an information board and follow the rampart around for about ¾ mile, passing through two gates.

4 **[ST 783989]** As **Cam Long Down** comes into view on the left (and in

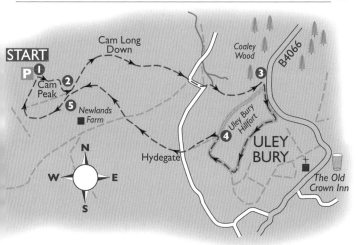

the distance **May Hill** and the **Malvern Hills**), turn sharply left over a stile and onto a footpath and begin a challenging descent towards **Hydegate**. When the path meets a metalled road junction go straight over passing the **Hydegate Pet Centre** to the right. Just after the Pet Centre turn right down a track and follow this until it meets another track. Turn right and go up the slope for about 150 metres and, as the lane sweeps around to the right, take the bridleway to the left.

[ST 769991] Follow the bridleway into the woods surrounding **Cam Peak** and follow the path which follows the perimeter of the peak in a clockwise direction to return to the car park.

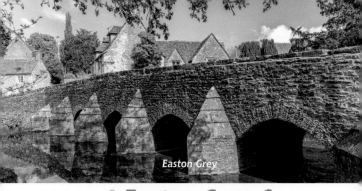

Easton Grey

4 Easton Grey & the Fosse Way
Echoes of the past
6 miles (9.5 km)

WALK HIGHLIGHTS
This is a walk full of history and birdsong as you meander along quiet lanes and ancient pathways. Signs of the Industrial Revolution can be seen in the remains of a former corn mill called Fosse Mill (still in use in 1870, but gone by 1900). The atmospheric Fosse Way, a section of Roman road, is moss covered and tranquil, as it passes the site of a Roman wayside settlement now under the protection of English Heritage. Pass through peaceful villages and along byways far from the busy hub of tourist areas.

THE WALK
1 **[ST 884876]** From the parking place enter the field on the southern side of the road and walk down to the valley. The footpath should go through the field but is not always clear. At the lower right-hand corner there is a gap in the hedge leading to the next field. Go through to join the **White Walls Way**. Keep to the right-hand edge of the field (ignore the first gap on the right-hand side seen after about 70 metres) continue to the next gap which has a path leading down to the infant **River Avon**. Cross the footbridge and pass the ruined industrial buildings of **Fosse Mill** which

spring

STARTING POINT & PARKING: Lay-by to the east of Easton Grey on the B4040, with a footpath sign pointing into the field. **Sat Nav:** SN16 0RD.

MAP: OS Explorer 168 Stroud, Tetbury & Malmesbury. **Grid Ref:** ST 884876. **what3words:** comply.recording.stump

TERRAIN: Some moderate inclines and field walking. Some quiet country roads and byways.

FOOD & DRINK: The Vine Tree, Foxley Road, Norton, Malmesbury, SN16 0JP. ☎ 01666 837654. A welcoming inn with a beamed bar area, cosy fire for the colder months and lovely terrace and garden for when the sun shines.

are on the southern side of the river. Walk up the footpath and along the edge of a field and a further footpath to reach a lane leading down to the river again.

[ST 889870] This emerges onto the **Fosse Way** by a bridge over the Avon (on the northern side of the river is the site of the Roman settlement). Go right and follow the track uphill. At the summit, and just before a metal barrier, there is a clearing and a gate on the left-hand side leading into a field marked as the **White Walls Way**. Follow this path as it passes around the edge of fields and a small wood eventually joining up with a track leading towards the hamlet of **Foxley**. As the track passes the corner of a field there is a small cairn with an enigmatic memorial stone containing a Roald Dahl quotation.

[ST 895859] The track emerges onto a road. Leave the White Walls Way and turn right and follow this road for about 100 metres to a fork – the road takes the right-hand fork and the other leads to the **Foxley Manor Farm** complex. On the left-hand side of the road is a stile. Cross over and follow the edge of the field around to a metal gate and stile. Go over the stile, turn left and follow the hedge on the left-hand side of the field. Follow this as it passes over two stiles and then go left over a third stile into a field. Turn right and follow the field edge around to a second field. Follow the footpath towards the village of **Norton**. The footpath emerges at the corner of the field and next to the **Vine Tree**.

spring

The Cotswolds Year Round Walks

④ [ST 887845]
Turn right onto
the road, head
past the pub and
down towards a
three-cross-way by
a stream. At this
junction take the
right-hand fork
uphill towards
Easton Grey.
After about 75
metres turn left
at a fingerpost and
follow this path.
By a converted
outbuilding, now
a private house,
follow the wooden
fence to skirt by
the southern edge
of some houses,
cross a stile into
a field. Just past
a disued mill,
take a stile on the
right into a field.
Follow the arrow
directions. Cross a
stile into a second
field, and again
follow the arrow directions, this time to the left-hand corner. Cross a
stile, go left and follow the field edge. Just as you enter the next field
there is a stile on the right onto a lane.

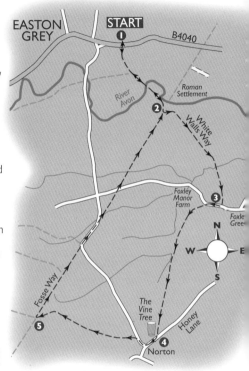

⑤ [ST 872845] This is the **Fosse Way**. Turn right and follow it back to the
crossing of the **River Avon** and then retrace your steps back past the
ruined mill to the parking place.

spring

Warden's Wood

5 Whittington & Belas Knap
Whispering woods and forgotten valleys

3¼ miles (5.2 km) or 5 miles (8 km) if taking the detour to Belas Knap

WALK HIGHLIGHTS

This is a secret walk, away from the more popular Cleeve Hill. Expect a charming mix of small valleys, high uplands, woodlands and wildlife far from the busy thoroughfares of its neighbours. In spring, the woods on the home straight are covered with bluebells, violets, daffodils and primroses. There is a steep hill towards the final stage, and the closing section requires some concentration; stick to the main path – if you miss the car park and reach the lane you only have to follow this back to reach the starting point. For those who want a longer walk, a ¾-mile extension beyond Wontley Farm brings you to Belas Knap, a Neolithic long barrow now under the care of English Heritage.

spring

The Cotswolds Year Round Walks

STARTING POINT & PARKING: Warden's Wood (aka West Down) car park, Cleeve Common. **Sat Nav:** GL54 5TN.

MAP: OS Explorer OL 45 The Cotswolds. **Grid Ref:** SP 009236.
  what3words: banquets.pegs.provide

TERRAIN: Moorland and woodland tracks (quite rutted in places), some quiet country lanes. Some gradients, one of which is quite steep.

FOOD & DRINK: The Craven Arms, Brockhampton, Cheltenham, GL54 5XQ. ☎ 01242 820410. A traditional 16th-century inn situated in the Cotswold countryside. There is a nice garden and a good choice of full meals and lighter options.

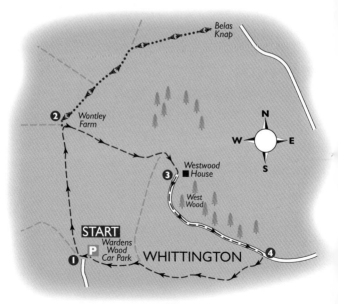

spring

THE WALK

[SP 009236] From the car park head north (away from the entry road) along a bridle way. This is quite a rutted track and is not the footpath to **Cleeve Common** which is through a kissing gate to the left.

[SP 008246] At the abandoned **Wontley Farm** turn right and follow the hill down to **Westwood House**. [There is the option at Wontley Farm to visit the prehistoric burial chamber of **Belas Knap**. Head straight up (north-east) the path at the crossing by Wontley Farm for about 400 metres and join the Cotswold Way to Belas Knap which is visible to the right. Return to Wontley Farm by reversing course.]

[SP 018243] At Westwood House follow the lane down through the valley for about ¾ mile.

[SP 025236] About 75 metres after a lodge (on the left) turn right onto the **Sabrina Way** and follow it uphill. Follow the path through the woods until it emerges back at the car park.

6 Snowshill & Lidcombe Wood

A tour or tures

4½ miles (7.2 km)

WALK HIGHLIGHTS

This is an 'up, down and up again' hill walk, not for the faint-hearted, but well worth the effort. It combines a wealth of history with peaceful woods and high panoramic views. The summer months showcase the elevated open spaces, while the woods (mainly beech with some hazel and ash) provide a cool canopy on hot days. Lidcombe Wood, mentioned in the *Domesday Book*, became a deer park in medieval times. It was enclosed by a wall, some of which survives and can be seen to this day. Tracks to several tures (walled routes to drive animals to water or market) are passed, offshoots from the main walk, and these justify a detour if time and energy allow. Despite the demands of the terrain at times, this is a rewarding walk that holds many secrets, its ancient history there for the finding.

20

STARTING POINT & PARKING: Lay-by. Drive through the small hamlet of Taddington towards Snowshill. Just after some open fields a rough lane joins from the left and by this junction is the lay-by. Sat Nav: GL54 5RY.

MAP: OS Explorer OL 45 The Cotswolds. Grid Ref: SP 090327. what3words: anchors.awoke.requests

TERRAIN: Sides of fields and woodland tracks, some of which are quite challenging. Some quiet roads.

FOOD & DRINK: The Snowshill Arms, Snowshill, Broadway, WR12 7JU. ☎ 01386 852653. An attractive 15th-century pub serving local beers and a good range of food from sandwiches to full meals that can be eaten inside or out in the large beer garden.

THE WALK

[SP 091328] From the parking place take the footpath into the woods in a westerly direction. Ignore the path running parallel to the road off to the left and follow the edge of the woods on the right-hand side. After about 100 metres this enters a field, continue to follow the hedge on the right-hand side.

[SP 084329] As the field ends, a crossing of paths and tracks is reached, turn left and walk down the lane. Turn right when the track meets a roughly metalled road. Follow the road for about 500 metres to a crossroads.

[SP 082316] At the crossroads turn right and follow the bridleway down through the woods for about a mile. As the woodland track ends, look left before re-entering the woods to see views across to **Dumbleton** and the hills beyond.

[SP 068321] At the bottom of this track turn right by a collection of cottages and walk up the footpath. After a short, sharp climb this descends to a clearing with a small building off to the left. This building has a set of information boards within and is worth visiting. *The clanking of a pump is also very apparent at this point and provides a clue to the early industrial heritage of the area. The many springs in the woods* once provided energy to fuel the mills, first fulling mills then a paper mill. Since 2004, along with help from the pump, they have powered the Stanway Fountain, the tallest gravity-fed fountain in the world, situated in the grounds of **Stanway House**, a mile or so away. Continue up the footpath, cross straight over a crossing of forest trails and continue up

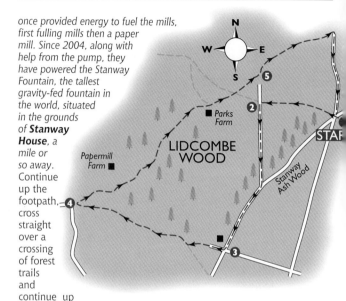

to a gate to emerge by the buildings of **Parks Farm**. Bear left and follow the track uphill; when the track veers off to the right go straight on through a gate and across two fields at a slight angle to emerge onto a footpath running north-south. *As higher ground is reached there are views across to distant countryside and then* **Snowshill** *appears, nestled in the hills.*

5 **[SP 084331]** Turn left onto the main path and after about 25 metres turn right downhill. After passing through two fields and crossing a track this path emerges onto a metalled road. Turn right onto the road and after about 100 metres turn right again and follow the footpath past a stable back to the parking place.

summer

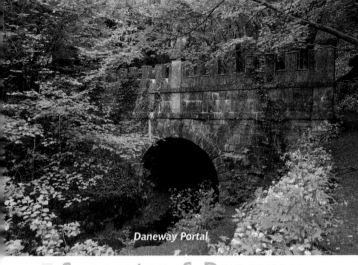

Daneway Portal

7 Sapperton & Daneway

Nature reclaimed

4½ miles (7.2 km)

WALK HIGHLIGHTS

Shortly after leaving Sapperton, the walk passes down and through a valley where the only sounds are running water from the crystal-clear streams, and the wind in the trees, interspersed by birdsong. Daneway Banks nature reserve is home to one of the biggest colonies of the large blue butterfly in the country. These can be seen flying during a brief window from late June to the beginning of July. In Siccaridge Wood, coppicing (where trees are cut to ground level) creates a dense shrub layer at the base of the tree, which helps the dormouse to thrive. This is ancient woodland, and the valley has many and varied wild flowers such as yellow flag irises, which can be seen growing from May onwards throughout the summer months. This walk also gives you the chance to see the remains of the Thames and Severn Canal. The canal was considered a great engineering feat mainly due to the skill in the construction of the Sapperton tunnel and the deep locks. Sadly, it was

The Cotswolds Year Round Walks

STARTING POINT & PARKING: Roadside, Church Lane in Sapperton, opposite the village school. Sat Nav: GL7 6LQ.

MAP: OS Explorer 168 Stroud, Tetbury & Malmesbury. Grid Ref: SO 946032. what3words: devoured.limped.because

TERRAIN: Forest trails and tracks with some demanding gradients.

FOOD & DRINK: The Bell, Sapperton, Cirencester, GL7 6LE. ☎ 01285 760298. You'll find flagstone floors, beamed ceilings, log fires and a wine shop inside this award-winning country inn. Food is seasonal and locally sourced where possible.
The Daneway Inn, Dane Lane, Sapperton, Cirencester, GL7 6LN. ☎ 01285 760297. A rustic looking inn with a large lawned garden and good-sized menu. There is also an outdoor café open at weekends serving coffee and sandwiches.

not profitable and it closed two hundred years after opening. Wildlife however has benefitted, and this is a lovely secluded stretch to wander along. This is a wonderfully peaceful and tranquil meander through nature with a taste of early industrial history.

THE WALK

1 **[SO 946032]** Walk along **Church Lane** towards the church. At the junction follow the **Macmillan Way** in a north-easterly direction for about a mile (in winter this can be muddy and churned up by horses).

2 **[SO 955044]** At the end of a field, leave the Macmillan Way and take the left-hand track (this is just before a gate) downhill into the valley and across the stream. There is a

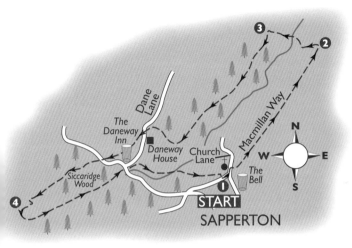

footbridge as well as a ford at this point. Just after the footbridge take the right fork and follow the track up the hill.

[SO 951045] Near the summit turn left and follow the woodland path westwards and emerge at a road (**Dane Lane**) near **Daneway House**. Cross over and follow the trail through **Daneway Banks nature reserve** (and past the seat to commemorate the visit of HRH The Prince of Wales) across the road and into **Siccaridge Wood**.

[SO 928030] Follow the trail through the wood to emerge onto the remains of the **Thames and Severn Canal**. Turn left onto a track and then immediately turn right over a bridge. On the far side of the bridge turn left onto the towpath. Follow the canal eastwards, passing several derelict locks before reaching the **Daneway Inn**. Continue to follow the footpath as it runs by the canal and when the tunnel mouth is reached follow the footpath over the tunnel to enter a meadow on the north-west side of **Sapperton**. Ascend the meadow and emerge near the school and parking place.

summer

8 Foxcote
Burials and birdsong

5½ miles (9 km)

WALK HIGHLIGHTS

Situated close to the A436, it is easy to miss this walk. The sound of the road quickly disappears, to be replaced by birdsong. Much of the site is unimproved red limestone grassland, rich in wild flowers, with over 100 different flowering plant species. There are 20 different species of butterfly, including the extremely rare Duke of Burgundy, which can be seen in May and June. Offering a variety of scenery, the geography of the area ranges from high hills to tranquil valleys and quiet woodland. At the outset is a mound with a cluster of trees known as 'St Paul's Epistle', originally a bowl barrow or ancient burial site. Shortly beyond this there are panoramic views towards Oxford, with woodlands scattered in the foreground. A steep walk downhill takes you through Foxcote, then uphill and back down into peaceful woodland. The final stretch returns the walker to high countryside, with open views on either side. Look out for birds of prey and hares in the fields to the left. Early morning in summer shows the walk at its best.

summer

STARTING POINT & PARKING: Kilkenny Viewpoint car park (also known as Cold Comfort Common). From the A436 take the minor road signposted 'Hilcot 2' and then turn immediately left into the car park. Sat Nav: GL54 4AX.

MAP: OS Explorer OL 45 The Cotswolds. Grid Ref: SP 004186.
what3words: steaming.umbrella.reverses

TERRAIN: Fields and woodland trails. Some quiet, metalled lanes.

FOOD & DRINK: **The Kilkeney Inn**, Andoversford Cheltenham, GL54 4LN. ☎ 01242 820341. Expect a warm welcome at this pretty country inn (originally five stone cottages). There is a choice of dining areas including a conservatory overlooking the garden. The menu consists of traditional pub grub, slow-cooked specials and sandwiches, which are available at lunchtime.

THE WALK

[SP 004186] Exit the car park via a kissing gate and head uphill through the site towards the mobile phone mast. Leave the site by another kissing gate and continue walking along the metalled road away from the main road, towards **Foxcote Hill Farm**. This takes you past the distinctive bowl barrow called '**St Paul's Epistle**'. Continue down the lane to where the **Gloucestershire Way** crosses it, and turn left into a field.

[SP 002179] Follow the Gloucestershire Way through a gate to the right and then turn left to go down a steep hill and, veering left at the bottom, follow the track in a north-east direction. After about 100 metres turn right at a waymark across a field and continue through a gate into a wooded area. The footpath passes through a riding stable and then emerges onto a metalled lane in the hamlet of **Foxcote**. Turn right and walk downhill. After about 15 metres turn left and just after the Gloucestershire Way passes through a gate leave it by turning right and walking downhill towards the corner of the field. Cross a stile and footbridge and follow the stream for about 10 metres to emerge onto a lane. Turn left and then almost immediately turn right into a field and walk up through this field to a gate and then turn left. Follow the contour through a couple of fields to a track which emerges at the entrance road to the **Thorndale Farm** complex.

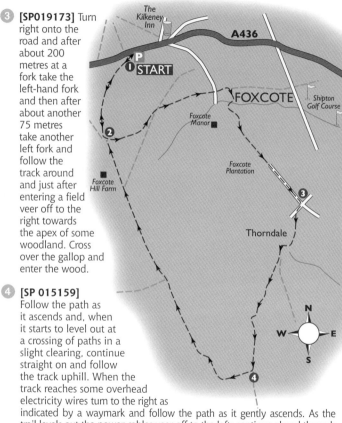

③ **[SP019173]** Turn right onto the road and after about 200 metres at a fork take the left-hand fork and then after about another 75 metres take another left fork and follow the track around and just after entering a field veer off to the right towards the apex of some woodland. Cross over the gallop and enter the wood.

④ **[SP 015159]** Follow the path as it ascends and, when it starts to level out at a crossing of paths in a slight clearing, continue straight on and follow the track uphill. When the track reaches some overhead electricity wires turn to the right as indicated by a waymark and follow the path as it gently ascends. As the trail levels out the power cables veer off to the left; continue ahead through several fields until the path reaches the Gloucestershire Way. Retrace the route to the **Kilkenny Viewpoint** parking space and recreational area.

View from the Macmillan Way

9 Yanworth

Forgotten history

5½ miles (9 km)

WALK HIGHLIGHTS

Footpaths close to the A40 are often overlooked, but to do so is to miss out on some of the best walks in the Cotswolds. This summer walk combines wide-open views with gentle valleys. Deer can sometimes be seen grazing in fields. The latter half of the walk is downhill to the Coln valley, looking across to wooded hills. The winding river passes the Old Mill and here the walk goes uphill to Yanworth, a quiet attractive collection of houses and converted barns. This relatively forgotten area offers peace and solitude. A short distance away from the roads and busy traffic, the only sounds you are likely to hear are the breeze in the trees and the river meandering nearby.

THE WALK

[SP 088151] Cross the road from the parking place and follow the **Macmillan Way** north-east towards **Hampnett**. After a stile, walk downhill to the valley floor and turn right away from the Macmillan

29

STARTING POINT & PARKING: Lay-by. From the A40 turn off at the sign for 'Yanworth 4 Compton Abdale 1½'. Follow this road towards Northleach and at a junction signposted 'Yanworth, Fossebridge and Coln St Dennis' there is a large lay-by on the right-hand side of the road, park here. Sat Nav: GL54 3QF.

MAP: OS Explorer OL 45 The Cotswolds. Grid Ref: SP 088151.
what3words: crusted.pouch.tolerates

TERRAIN: Field paths and tracks, some quiet lanes. Some moderately challenging gradients.

FOOD & DRINK: **The Wheatsheaf Inn**, West Road, Northleach, Cheltenham, GL54 3EZ. ☎ 01451 860244. A cosy 17th-century coaching inn with an attractive bar and dining area, as well as a lovely terraced garden.

Way. Follow the valley floor until the path reaches the **Monarch's Way**. Turn right to join the Monarch's Way and proceed in a southerly direction rising uphill and then crossing a road. Continue straight on across the field with a small stone wall on the right.

2 **[SP 095141]** At the reservoir, cross the road and take the path to the right which leads across a field towards **Oxpens Farm**. Do not enter the farm but turn to the left through a gate before the track reaches the farm buildings. Walk along the edge of a field with a wood on the right for about ½ mile – the path is gently descending at this stage. When the footpath meets a metalled road turn right and walk downhill. At the bottom of the hill where the road sweeps around to the right, go straight ahead on a footpath which tracks along the course of the river towards **Yanworth Mill**.

3 **[SP 072130]** At the mill leave the Monarch's Way, turn right and walk up the road towards **Yanworth**. After about 500 metres turn right into a field at a fingerpost and follow a footpath leading across this field to the left of an enclosed, circular clump of trees. Pass through a gate and, with the imposing **Yanworth House** to the right, carry on to the road. Turn right and after about 100 metres, where the road turns to the right, take a left and then almost immediately a right downhill to the church on the Macmillan Way. Walk through the churchyard and out through the gate at the north-east corner. Walk down to meet a metalled road, turn left and follow it downhill passing a curious circular water feature on the way. Continue uphill and as the road begins to level out take a left turn at a fingerpost.

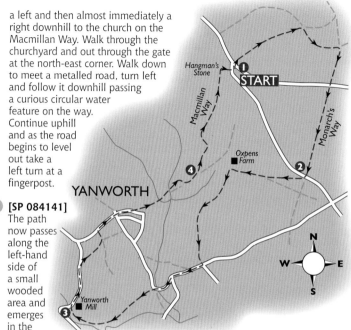

[SP 084141] The path now passes along the left-hand side of a small wooded area and emerges in the farmyard of **Oxpens Farm**. Turn left and follow the Macmillan Way which now tracks along the left-hand side of a field with a wooded grove to the left. At the top of the hill by the **Hangman's Stone** is a fingerpost which indicates the way back to the road and the starting point. *The origins of the Hangman's Stone are unknown. It is said to be two stones. One tale describes a sheep rustler who tripped climbing the stile and became entangled with the dead animal! It may even have been part of a gibbet. In days gone by those found guilty of a crime and sentenced to death were often returned to a place close to the scene of the crime to be hanged. But the original purpose of the stone remains unclear. Nowadays the only activity to be seen is a friendly robin who seems unperturbed by the mystery of the stone's past.*

31

Aldsworth Village

10 Aldsworth
A breath of fresh air

6 miles (9.5 km)

WALK HIGHLIGHTS

This is an elevated walk with breathtaking views across mainly level and gentle terrain, ideal for warm summer days. From Saxon times the land around Aldsworth was unenclosed sheep pasture, and an open field system was in practice until 1973. This lack of historical enclosure appears to be reflected today in the expanse of open countryside seen on the walk. In the village is the first clue to the connection the area has with the Second World War. Opposite the war memorial, on a nearby gate is a plaque to Flight Lieutenant Geoffrey Roscoe, a 25-year-old Battle of Britain pilot who was fatally injured when his plane crashed in a nearby field in 1942. Further on, at the preserved control tower on the old airfield, is another memorial plaque dedicated to Flight Sergeant Bruce Hancock. He lost his life by deliberately crashing his plane into a German aircraft. Today transport aircraft from RAF Brize Norton occasionally fly overhead.

32

STARTING POINT & PARKING: Lay-by on the B4425. 100 metres to the west of the Sherborne Arms there is large parking area on the left-hand side of the main road. Sat Nav: GL54 3RB.

MAP: OS Explorer OL 45 The Cotswolds. Grid Ref: SP 157099. what3words: luggage.chainsaw.softest

TERRAIN: Field edges and farm tracks. Some road walking – mostly along quiet lanes but about 100 metres of busier road. Gentle gradients.

FOOD & DRINK: **The Sherborne Arms**, Aldsworth, Cheltenham, GL54 3RB, ☎ 01451 844346. A 16th-century family-owned traditional pub where you can expect good food and a warm welcome.

THE WALK

[SP 157099] From the lay-by cross the road and walk into the village of **Aldsworth**. Pass around the right-hand side of the grassy triangle by the war memorial. Carry on up the road to the footpath sign to the right by **Sandles Cottage**. Follow this eastward out of the village past a small copse and then into a field and turn right. Follow the right-hand edge of the field until you reach a place where the path appears to fall over a steep slope. Descend the slope and turn left (north-easterly) and follow the path to **Budgehill Wood**. Bear away from the path towards a gap in the wall and then follow the left-hand edge of the field to the intersection by **Windrush Camp** (**Camp Barn**).

[SP 180123] Turn sharp right and follow the path past a farmhouse and onto the site of the former **RAF Windrush**. Proceed across the airfield to a fingerpost and then turn right. It can be difficult to see the fingerpost but if you look for a clump of evergreen trees in the middle distance and aim for the right-hand edge of this clump the fingerpost eventually comes into view. Follow the rudimentary hedgerow until it meets a track; follow this track in the same direction. After about 400 metres turn left and descend past the ruins of **Lower Barn**. Turn right at the edge of the trees and follow the track to the road (B4425).

[SP 178101] Turn right and walk along the road for about 100 metres and then cross over and take the footpath towards **Ladbarrow Farm**.

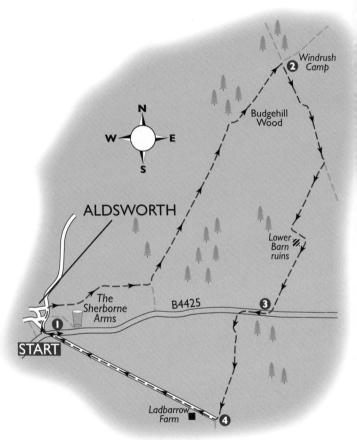

4 **[SP 172091]** Turn right and follow the lane back to the parking place,

The Reading Room

11 Edgeworth & Ruscombe Plantation
Hidden history

4 miles (6.5 km)

WALK HIGHLIGHTS

The ancient parish of Edgeworth is located by a steep wooded valley. At the outset, the route rambles along lanes and fields, before descending into woodland. Autumn shows the trees and wildlife at their best. Deer and badgers find shelter here, along with a wide variety of birds. There are some steep uphill and downhill stretches, interspersed with open fields, but on the whole this is an enclosed route. Far away from the bustle and noise of modern-day life, this is a route with its own pleasing

autumn

The Cotswolds Year Round Walks

STARTING POINT & PARKING: Parking area on School Lane by Edgeworth Reading Room. 100 metres to the west of the Sherborne Arms there is large parking area on the left-hand side of the main road. **Sat Nav:** GL6 7JQ.

MAP: OS Explorer 179 Gloucester, Cheltenham & Stroud. **Grid Ref:** SO 946063. **what3words:** blanks.snacks.skylights

TERRAIN: Field and country tracks, a short distance along a quiet road. Two moderate-to-steep gradients.

FOOD & DRINK: The Carpenters Arms, Miserden, Stroud GL6 7JA. ☎ 01285 821283. A traditional village pub where produce is sourced locally or grown in their own kitchen garden. As well as a good lunch menu, breakfast is served from 9am and the afternoon tea makes for a perfect post-walk treat.

soundscape. As well as the birdsong and the wind in the trees, there is the babble of water from nearby streams, not least the Holy Brook which runs through the valley of the same name.

THE WALK

1 [SO 946063] Walk back up from the **Reading Room** to the main road, turn left and, at a Y-junction, take the right-hand fork towards the **Miserden** road and go straight across. Follow the footpath down the side of a field and descend into the woods.

2 [SO 934069] At a Y-junction take the left fork and follow the contour around to emerge at **Monsell Cottage**. Walk down the steep hill, cross the stream and then fork left towards **Througham Slad**.

3 [SO 926064] Cross over two stiles and emerge at a three cross way of tracks. Take the track straight ahead down the hill (the left-hand track leads to a large house and the right-hand track goes uphill to the hamlet of **Througham Slad**). Walk down the track and up the other side. As the track sweeps around to the right, about halfway up the hill, turn left through the field and follow the footpath to reach another track.

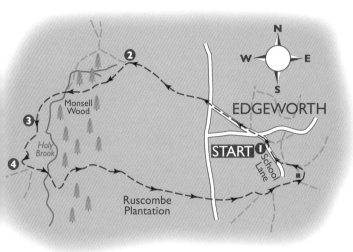

[SO 926062] Turn left and follow this track into the valley floor and then zig-zag up. Leaving the valley behind, pause halfway up the track to look down at the lake, easily overlooked tucked away as it is on the valley edge. After a group of estate buildings on the left continue to the crest for about 100 metres. At the crest of the hill take the bridleway to the right through a gate and into a small wooded area and follow this bridleway along the field edges to the road. Go straight over and follow the bridleway downhill and past the cottages before emerging at the church. *Arriving back at* **Edgeworth**, *the dramatic façade of the 17th-century manor can be seen to the right.* Pass through the churchyard and follow the path to emerge at the old school house, turn right and follow the road back up the hill to the **Reading Room**. *Reading Rooms were first introduced in the mid-19th century, created for the working class by philanthropic landowners.*

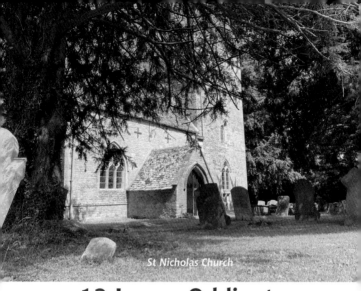
St Nicholas Church

12 Lower Oddington & Bledington
Religion, railways and rural peace
4¾ miles (7.5 km)

WALK HIGHLIGHTS

At the start of the walk is the church of St Nicholas at Lower Oddington. This dates from the 12th century and is famous for a Doom painting (a wall painting of the Last Judgement) which, at 32 feet long and 15 feet high, is possibly the largest example of a medieval church wall painting in Britain. Look out for marks on the stone seats in the porch – these were made by medieval archers who sharpened their arrowheads before leaving their weapons outside and going in to the service. On the way to Bledington, the walk passes through woodland, lanes and fields, all full of birdsong. In Autumn, the trees provide seasonal colour and their canopy protection from the elements, while the lanes make for easier

STARTING POINT & PARKING: Roadside, Church Road. There are some parking spaces near St Nicholas Church, Lower Oddington. **Sat Nav:** GL56 0UP.

MAP: OS Explorer OL 45 The Cotswolds. **Grid Ref:** SP 234255.
   what3words: passports.publish.hazy

TERRAIN: Woodland tracks and trails, field edges and paths through waterside pasture. Almost no gradients to contend with but underfoot conditions can be waterlogged after wet weather.

FOOD & DRINK: The King's Head Inn, The Green, Bledington, OX7 6XQ. ☎ 01608 658365. Award-winning inn situated in the picturesque village of Bledington. Ingredients are locally sourced and seasonal.

walking. Further along is the River Evenlode, where willows grow on the banks and swans and herons can be seen. Be warned: during bad weather this stage can get very wet and muddy. The area has always been prone to this, the result of heavy clay soil which inhibits drainage.

THE WALK

[SP 234255] Head south (away from the village) along the track from the church. After about 1 mile the track veers to the right. At this point enter the woodland through a gate and immediately turn right. Follow this path for about 100 metres through the wooded area and then emerge onto a concreted farm track, turn left and follow the footpath waymarks. The path runs down the left-hand side of some fields for about a mile before turning left over a stile to join a track. Follow the track southwards. After about 500 metres it crosses the old railway line.

[SP 244232] 30 metres further on (just before a concrete bridge over a stream) turn left into a field. Follow the footpath into the village of Bledington and turn left when emerging onto a street. Follow this lane which eventually enters a field. Turn left to follow the edge of the field around to a footbridge and then over the old railway line – you have now joined the **Seven Shires Way**.

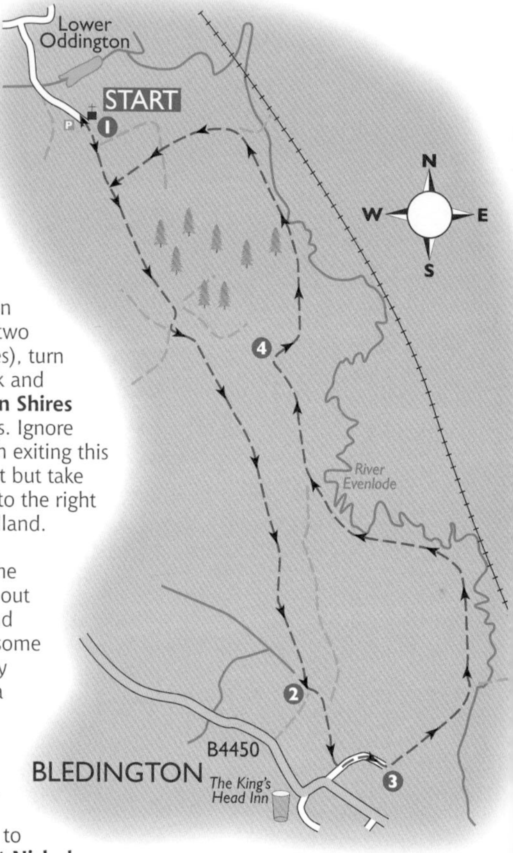

The Cotswolds Year Round Walks

③ [SP 250231]
Follow the footpath northwards as it traces the course of the twisty **River Evenlode**. After about a mile it enters a wooded area (under a wooden arch formed of two interlocking trees), turn right at the track and follow the **Seven Shires Way** northwards. Ignore the first footpath exiting this track to the right but take the second exit to the right out of the woodland.

④ [SP 242245] The path turns right out of the woods and passes through some fields, eventually emerging onto a concreted farm track. Turn left and follow the track uphill to a T-junction. Turn right and return to the **church of St Nicholas**.

Lower Oddington

START

BLEDINGTON

B4450

The King's Head Inn

River Evenlode

autumn

Buckholt Wood

13 Cranham & Cooper's Hill
Up and down, high and low

4 miles (6.5 km)

WALK HIGHLIGHTS

The first and last stages of this walk are through Buckholt Wood, ancient woodland thought to have existed here since just after the last Ice Age. Beech is the most common tree along with ash, oak, wych elm and alder, providing autumnal colour both overhead and underfoot. Deer, fox and badger make their home here, and in autumn goldcrests, tits and treecreepers are just a few of the varieties of birdlife you might see. Cooper's Hill Nature Reserve is on the edge of the escarpment, and in autumn the dense moist beech woodland is particularly beautiful with its canopy of leaves changing colour. There is the option of diverting to the Great Witcombe Roman Villa before the return leg through Buckholt Wood.

41

The Cotswolds Year Round Walks

STARTING POINT & PARKING: Buckholt Wood Car Park. **Sat Nav:** GL4 8HB.

MAP: Explorer 179 Gloucester, Cheltenham & Stroud. **Grid Ref:** SO 893131. **what3words:** limitless.observers.chromatic

TERRAIN: Woodland paths and trails. Some steep gradients.

FOOD & DRINK: The Royal William, Cheltenham Road, Cranham, GL6 6TT. ☎ 01452 813650. A traditional country pub where the staff are friendly and the food is good.

THE WALK

1 **[SO 893131]** Stand in the car park with your back to the road and face the wood. Take the middle path at about 10 o'clock up the hill for about ½ mile. When this emerges onto the metalled road cross right over and continue uphill for ¼ mile. Join up with the **Cotswold Way** and follow it in the northerly direction, initially negotiating a steep descent before walking gradually up the path to the summit of the cheese rolling slope. *The Cooper's Hill Cheese-Rolling and Wake is an annual event. A round of Double Gloucester cheese is rolled down the steep hill as competitors run after it with the aim of catching it. The custom may have evolved from an ancient requirement for maintaining grazing rights, although it has also been linked to pagan customs, when bundles of burning brushwood were rolled down the hill to welcome the birth of the New Year.*

2 **[SO 891147]** Descend **Cooper's Hill** to the left (west) of the slope turning right at the bottom to emerge at the foot of the hill and continue to the right along the **Cotswold Way**. After about ¾ mile there is a spur off to the left to the **Great Witcombe Roman Villa** which is worth a visit if time allows. *In a peaceful setting, this was once a large and opulent Roman villa built around AD 250. There are the remains of a bathhouse complex as well as what is believed to be the shrine of a water spirit. A modern building, not open to the casual visitor, contains mosaic flooring.*

3 **[SO 903137]** Pass the villa signpost and continue along the **Cotswold Way** for about ¼ mile. Ignore an unmarked path bearing off to the right but after another 75 metres turn to the right when you can

42

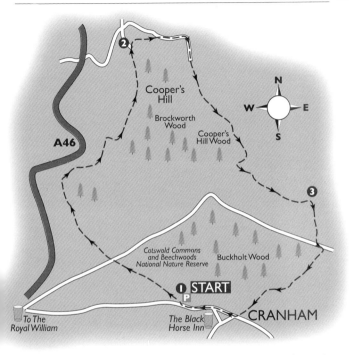

see a large house peering out of the trees and follow the footpath (waymarked as the Cotswolds Way circular) right and up the hill to the road. Cross over and take the footpath sign left marked 'Cotswolds Way circular' (ignore the footpath further up to the right). After 20 metres, at another fingerpost, go right into woods and a small car park. In the car park take the roughly metalled road downhill (this lane is an extension of the lane entering the car park), past a house called **Monk's Ditch** where the metalled surface ends. Cross the footbridge and emerge onto **Cranham Common**. At the road turn right and keep walking until you return to the car park on the right.

autumn

The former airfield

14 Chedworth
Time travel in Chedworth
3½ miles (5.5 km)

WALK HIGHLIGHTS

This autumn walk passes through three time periods as it winds across an open plateau, down into small valleys and steeply uphill again. The former airfield, built during the Second World War, dominates the immediate landscape; the Victorian railway line, closed in the 1960s, is now a nature reserve; and thirdly there is the Roman villa, with its wealth of archaeological finds.

 The walk starts at the former airfield, a haunt for birds of prey (as well as manmade kites!) and small mammals. Leaving the airfield behind, the walk continues downhill through woods rich in moss and lichen, the latter an indicator of the air quality. The woods and lower parts of the walk provide respite from the higher (sometimes bracing and windy) stages that come later, as well as showcasing striking autumnal leaf colour. Just past the railway bridge, up a few steps on the right, is the old railway line with fern-drenched banks on either side. Returning to the route, you pass the villa, and then begin the ascent on the latter

44

STARTING POINT & PARKING: Roadside, RAF Chedworth (disused). Do not veer off to the right to enter the village of Chedworth (signposted 'Lower Chedworth') but pass along its southern border to emerge at a four cross way. On the right are the remains of RAF Chedworth, a Second World War airfield. Take the right turn just prior to a triangular island (signposted 'Compton Abdale') and park on the left-hand side of the road before a sharp right-angled bend. **Sat Nav:** GL54 4NU.

MAP: OS Explorer OL 45 The Cotswolds. **Grid Ref:** SP 038131.
  what3words: dude.blotches.reserve

TERRAIN: Woodland tracks and trails with some steepish parts. Established footpaths.

FOOD & DRINK: The Seven Tuns, Queen Street, Chedworth, Cheltenham, GL54 4AE. ☎ 01285 720630. A 17th-century pub with an extensive wine cellar and locally brewed ales. Ingredients are locally sourced and food is served in the converted barn or on the attractive garden terrace.

stages. The exertion required here is rewarded by views across verdant fields and valleys to the airfield beyond. Haunting and atmospheric, this is a walk that will stay in your memory long after you leave.

THE WALK

[SP 038131] There are two public footpaths leading into the airfield from the road, both at sharp right-angled bends. These footpaths combine after about 100 metres, follow this in a south-easterly direction and then at a stile turn left along a farm track.

[SP 043128] At a small copse on the right-hand side, keep left on the track, and continue to follow the footpath as it branches off to the right and down through the woods. Eventually it passes underneath a disused railway bridge. Immediately after the bridge there are some steps to the right which lead up to the **Chedworth Nature Reserve**, which is the old railway line and worth a diversion. Continuing on the main route, the path now passes the entrance to **Chedworth Roman Villa**, owned by the National Trust. Walk down the lane and enter the car park.

autumn

The Cotswolds Year Round Walks

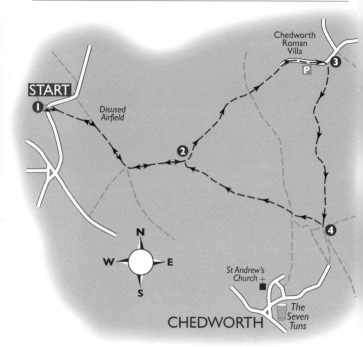

3 [SP 055133] On the track by the entrance gate to the car park is a gate off to the valley marked as the **Monarch's Way**. Follow this path as it ascends through the woods and emerges at a crossing of footpaths to the north of the village of **Chedworth**.

4 [SP 053125] Turn right and head back towards the disused airfield. The path passes a memorial bench on the right which is sited within a small copse. Re-join the footpath which passes around the perimeter of the former airfield and then turn right at a crossing of paths into the airfield to retrace your steps back to the parking place.

15 Somerford Keynes
Water, wildlife and rural reflections

5½ miles (9 km)

WALK HIGHLIGHTS

There are some short stretches of road at the start, but these soon disappear to be replaced by the sound and sights of water and birds. The River Thames features both at the start and end of the route. In autumn, bulrushes, lapwings and the occasional water vole may be seen along the way and the variety of birds and trees make this walk ideal for aspiring ornithologists and dendrologists. On a misty morning, the lakes have a solitary and atmospheric quality highlighted by the reflections on the water. It is worth a detour to Shorncote Church, built in 1170 when Norman lords were required to erect churches on their new estates. Ridge and furrow is evident in nearby fields.

autumn

The Cotswolds Year Round Walks

STARTING POINT & PARKING: Neigh Bridge Country Park car park. **Sat Nav:** GL7 6DU.

MAP: OS Explorer 169 Cirencester & Swindon. **Grid Ref:** SU 018947. **what3words:** daily.hems.crossings

TERRAIN: Flat lakeside and riverside paths, trails and tracks. Some very slight gradients along the edges of and through fields.

FOOD & DRINK: The Baker's Arms, Somerford Keynes, Cirencester, GL7 6DN. ☎ 01285 861298. An attractive family-run village pub serving seasonal and locally sourced produce. There is a good sized main menu but also a lunch menu with sandwiches and salads. There is an open fireplace inside and a nice garden for warmer days.

THE WALK

1 **[SU 018947]** Leave the car park via the entrance and at the junction with the road bear left towards **Somerford Keynes**. After about 100 metres turn right into **Mill Lane**. Follow this to the end and then cross the main road and follow the **Thames Path**. Continue along the Thames Path for about 1¼ miles, ignoring the "No Access" signs (the "No Access" refers to access to the **Lower Mill Estate**).

2 **[SU 036941]** Turn left at a footbridge and after about 200 metres, when the trail emerges onto a clearing, go straight on and follow the path to the road. Cross over and enter the **Cotswold Community** and follow the footpath in a northerly direction through the Community and into the gravel pit workings. *The Cotswold Community was established in 1941 as an approved school for boys from difficult backgrounds. It closed in 2013 and there are plans to build housing on the site.*

3 **[SU 033962]** At a T-junction turn left and cross over the conveyer belt via a footbridge. Follow the footpath as it skirts the lakes. At a grassy clearing continue straight on and then turn right and follow the footpath into some woods and out, past the **Shorncote Farm** buildings, to the road. Cross over and follow the footpath as it runs parallel to the road, emerging at a stile.

4 **[SU 023964]** Cross over and bear left. After about 50 metres enter a

48

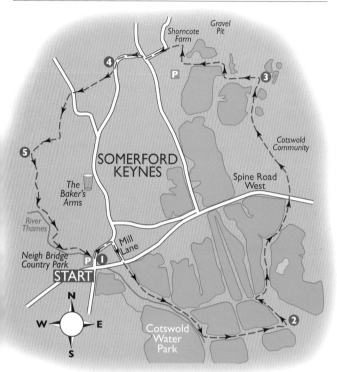

field on the right-hand side of the road and follow the hedge as the path gently ascends to a road. Cross the road and enter another field. Follow the path which runs diagonally across this field and at the far corner, at a fingerpost, turn right into another field. Follow the path across this field until it reaches the river (the infant **River Thames**).

[SU 012956] Turn left and follow the **Thames Path** back to the **Neigh Bridge Country Park** car park,

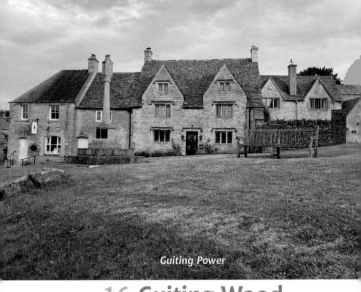
Guiting Power

16 Guiting Wood
A walk in the past
4½ miles (7.2 km)

WALK HIGHLIGHTS

The name Guiting derives from the Saxon word 'getinge', meaning rushing or outpouring of water. Set in an area rich in history, this walk provides both shelter and relatively dry paths, making it suitable for the winter. Initially it meanders along adjacent to a stream, before passing the ruins of a watermill and leading into peaceful woodlands. A short diversion allows you to see Black John's Pool. Its haunting name and appearance belies its probable mundane function as a cattle pool. The latter stretch of the walk opens up with softly undulating countryside on either side. The nearby village of Guiting Power, owned and managed by the Guiting Manor Amenity Trust, boasts a shop, bakery, post office and two pubs.

50

STARTING POINT & PARKING: Guiting Manor Amenity Trust car park. **Sat Nav:** GL54 5UZ.

MAP: OS Explorer OL 45 The Cotswolds. **Grid Ref:** SP 084258. **what3words:** relatives.graver.prefect

TERRAIN: Quiet lanes and woodland tracks with moderate gradients.

FOOD & DRINK: The Hollow Bottom, Guiting Power, Cheltenham, GL54 5UX, ☎ 01451 611111. An attractive 17th-century pub serving British classics. Locally sourced ingredients are served in a choice of areas inside or on the decked terrace outside.

THE WALK

[SP 084258] From the car park walk straight across the lane (i.e. north-west) to pass **Pump Bottom Cottage** and follow the **Winchcombe Way** up through the valley along a roughly metalled track (this is also part of the **Diamond Way**). The footprint of an old mill and millpond can be seen from the track.

[SP 079270] At the T-junction at the end of this track turn left and follow the road uphill for about a mile. Where the road veers off to the right go left to enter the **Farmcote Estate** and immediately turn to the right following the track, continue westwards (and then south-west) on the periphery of the wood. Where a footpath crosses the track, continue straight on and gently uphill. The track terminates at a T-junction of tracks but the footpath continues straight on (but slightly to the left) through the woods and emerges onto a road.

winter

3 **[SP 065258]** At this point a short detour of about 100 metres to the left will take the walker to **Black John's Pool** which can be seen through the hedge on the left-hand side of the road. Return to where the path emerges onto the road and continue straight over, down the track past **Newtown Farm** to emerge at **Roel Cottages** – the bridleway has an electrically operated gate.

4 **[SP 073249]** Turn left onto the lane and after about 400 metres go straight over the crossroads to continue back to the car park.

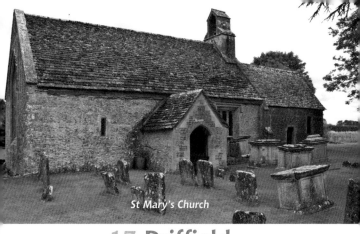
St Mary's Church

17 Driffield
A bird's-eye view
5 miles (8 km)

WALK HIGHLIGHTS

This is a walk through peaceful fields and along quiet lanes, the latter making for easy winter walking. Birds of prey fly overhead, along with skylarks in the open fields, even in winter. In point 1 small herds of deer are often seen. Approaching Ampney Crucis, the route crosses Ampney Brook (a tributary of the River Thames) which is then followed intermittently for some two miles. The church at Ampney St Mary stands adjacent to the site of a deserted medieval village, probably devastated by the Black Death in the 1300s. The village was moved to higher ground a mile or two away, the last houses being finally abandoned in the 18th century. In 1913, after years of decay, the ivy that covered the church was cleared away and it was thereafter dubbed 'the ivy church'. It is beautifully simple and atmospheric, with medieval wall paintings and a Norman tympanum. The latter is a stone carving over the old north door. It depicts the lion and two-headed snake, (representing good and evil) and a griffin (strength against evil) and is unique in England. Further on is 16th-century Harnhill Manor, now a centre of Christian healing set in parkland, before an easy walk back to the car.

53

The Cotswolds Year Round Walks

STARTING POINT & PARKING: Lay-by. From Ampney Crucis. take the lane opposite the pub on the A417 (signposted 'Harnhill and Driffield'). In ¾ mile turn left at the T-junction, and in a further ½ mile park in the lay-by on the left, by the entrance to a field. **Sat Nav:** GL7 5SQ.

MAP: OS Explorer 169 Cirencester & Swindon, Fairford & Cricklade. **Grid Ref:** SP 072009. **what3words:** terminology.tallest.clearcut

TERRAIN: Field edges, quiet lanes and tracks and woodland trails – muddy after wet weather.

FOOD & DRINK: The Lakeside Brasserie, The Watermark, Station Rd, South Cerney, GL7 5TH. ☎ 01285 860606. Although this is a 10-minute drive from the start of the walk, it is a popular spot in a lovely setting. Ingredients are locally sourced and there is a large menu to suit all tastes.

THE WALK

1 **[SP 072009]** With your back to lay-by, turn right and walk towards Harnhill. After 100 metres you'll reach a fingerpost, turn right into a field and then right again towards a gap in the hedge. Do not pass through but turn left and follow the hedge for 75 metres and turn right to pass through a gap in the hedge over a small bridge. Follow the hedge on the right across three fields in the direction of **Ampney Crucis**.

2 **[SP 071014]** About 150 metres before the road, turn right into a field and follow the path to a small church (**St Mary's at Ampney St Mary**). Cross the bridge and pass the church, aiming for the corner of the field by the road. Cross the A417 and follow the pavement for just under ½ mile.

3 **[SP 081013]** Cross again by the bus stop and walk down the lane, follow this for about 1¼ miles in the direction of **Down Ampney**. At **Charlham Farm House** the lane turns into a track. About ½ mile past the farm house, and just after entering a clump of trees, look for a fingerpost (which may be overgrown with ivy) on the right of the path.

4 **[SU 087995]** Turn right and follow the path over a bridge and through woods. On emerging turn right along the edge of the field. After 40 metres

54

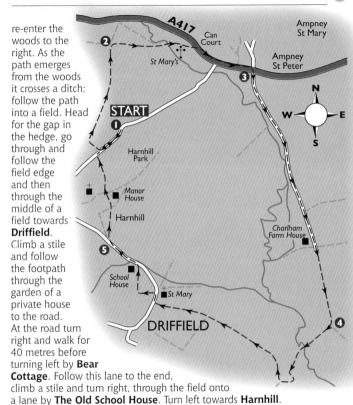

re-enter the woods to the right. As the path emerges from the woods it crosses a ditch; follow the path into a field. Head for the gap in the hedge, go through and follow the field edge and then through the middle of a field towards **Driffield**. Climb a stile and follow the footpath through the garden of a private house to the road. At the road turn right and walk for 40 metres before turning left by **Bear Cottage**. Follow this lane to the end, climb a stile and turn right, through the field onto a lane by **The Old School House**. Turn left towards **Harnhill**.

[SP 071001] After 200 metres enter a field to the right via a gate and take the right-hand of the two paths indicated by the fingerpost. Leave the field, cross a track and enter a field straight ahead. Immediately turn to the left and walk towards the road. Leave this field by a stile and turn right into a lane and return to the car.

winter

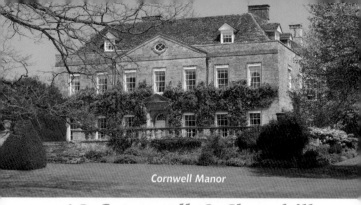

Cornwell Manor

18 Cornwell & Churchill
Hidden gems

5½ miles (9 km)

WALK HIGHLIGHTS

This is a peaceful walk, well off the beaten track. It can be muddy in places, but the quiet lanes and tracks make for easier winter walking. Although there is little woodland on the route, there are plenty of trees bordering the lanes and fields (mainly common alder and beech), plus the parkland at Cornwell Manor with a selection of oak, ash and beech. The Grade II-listed 16th-century manor was restored in 1939 by Clough Williams Ellis, who also remodelled the village cottages. Further on in the walk, at Churchill, there is a memorial to William Smith, considered the father of British geology, who was born here. The walk then passes through fields with lovely views across open landscape and the Evenlode Valley. Stow-on-the-Wold, its church spire often clearly visible, can be seen in the distance.

THE WALK

1 **[SP 270272]** From the parking spot, head back down the lane (south) through **Cornwell**. At the T-junction turn left and walk towards the entrance of **Cornwell Manor**. Just before the entrance, on the opposite side of the road, is a kissing gate and a fingerpost denoting two footpaths, follow the left-hand fork, which is the **D'Arcy-Dalton Way**, through **Hill Farm** and then through a sliding gate. As the farm road sweeps around to the right

56

STARTING POINT & PARKING: Roadside. On entering Cornwell village from the west, just after a lay-by and bus stop on the left, turn left and follow the road as it drops down and then rises up. As the road sweeps around to the left there is a grassy triangle with a signpost indicating the church to the right. Park against the hedge. **Sat Nav:** OX7 6TT.

MAP: OS Explorer 169 Cirencester & Swindon, Fairford & Cricklade. **Grid Ref:** SP 270272. **what3words:** bitter.tokens.twilight

TERRAIN: Field edges and paths, wide bridleways and some quiet country lanes. Some moderate gradients.

FOOD & DRINK: The Greedy Goose, Salford Hill, A44, Chastleton, Moreton-in-Marsh, GL56 0SP. ☎ 01608 646551. You can expect good food and friendly staff at this cosy village pub. Local ales are served along with a good selection of wines.

leave it and take the track to the left, following the left-hand hedge of a field. About halfway down look out for a footpath running diagonally off to the lower right-hand corner of this field and follow it to a bridleway.

[SP 277257] Leave the **D'Arcy-Dalton Way** by turning right into the bridleway which runs along the floor of the valley and follow it to where it meets a lane. Go straight on for about 250 metres and follow the road around the left-hand bend, past the old mill and then uphill past the site of the former **Sarsden Halt** into **Churchill**.

[SP 282243] Just before the T-junction, by the memorial to geologist William Smith, take the bridleway to the left and follow this past some stables, through some fields and wooded areas until you reach the rear entrance to **Churchill Grounds Farm**. Here, the bridleway becomes a track. Follow this to the lane.

[SP 286260] Turn left and walk over the bridges. Take the next right and after approximately 100 metres turn left along a bridleway. When this emerges at a lane, turn right and then right again at a junction. After about 300 metres (opposite **Glebe Farm**) turn left, and follow the footpath back to the church and on to the parking place.

winter

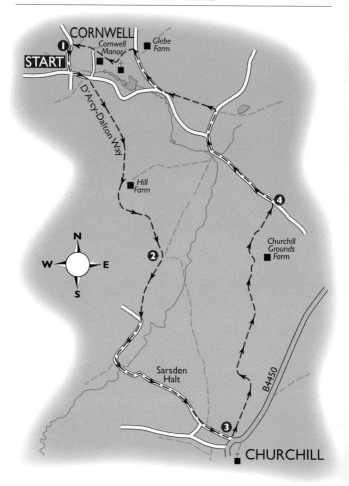

CORNWELL

START

Cornwell Manor

Glebe Farm

D'Arcy-Dalton Way

Hill Farm

2

N
W   E
S

4

Churchill Grounds Farm

Sarsden Halt

B4450

3

CHURCHILL

winter

Ebrington Village

19 Hidcote Manor & Ebrington
Valleys and vistas
5 miles (8 km)

WALK HIGHLIGHTS

The initial track up from the starting point with sweeping views back across to Chipping Campden provides a taste of what is to come. Further on, just beyond Ebrington Hill Farm, there is a wide panorama that takes in Brailes Hill and then Chipping Campden again (this time from a different vantage point). The bare trees silhouetted against the winter sky are a striking feature of the landscape, and this is an exhilarating stretch before the downhill drop to Ebrington. The village has a 13th-century church and 17th-century pub. An archaeological dig in the early 1900s uncovered the remains of a Roman villa. Ridge and furrow (medieval plough workings) is clearly visible in fields in stage 3. Buildings in Ebrington and Hidcote use the local stone with the rich golden colour typical of the north Cotswolds.

The Cotswolds Year Round Walks

STARTING POINT & PARKING: Hidcote National Trust car park. **Sat Nav:** GL55 6LP.

MAP: OS Explorer 205 Stratford-upon-Avon & Evesham. **Grid Ref:** SP 177430. **what3words:** salaried.boating.statement

TERRAIN: Field edges, paths and tracks. Some quiet lanes. Moderate gradients.

FOOD & DRINK: The Ebrington Arms, May Lane, Ebrington, Chipping Campden, GL55 6NH. ☎ 01386 593223. This award-winning inn, situated in an attractive village and surrounded by glorious countryside, is popular with locals and visitors alike. Food is seasonal, locally sourced where possible, and served by friendly staff.

The warm hue brings a welcome glow to a dull winter's day. This is an invigorating winter walk with spectacular scenery.

THE WALK

1 **[SP 177430]** At the entrance to the National Trust car park, head east up a rough track by a fingerpost, designated 'Restricted Byway'. Follow this track past some radio masts and buildings, cross over a metalled road and follow the footpath downhill to a road. Turn right onto the road and walk for about 200 metres in a south-westerly direction up a slight rise to a gate on the left.

2 **[SP 191423]** Turn left onto a bridleway for approximately 100 metres. When the bridleway veers to the left continue straight on along an indicated footpath in a south-westerly direction across a field. It is sometimes difficult to see exactly where this path runs but aim for a gap in the closest hedge. Follow this path downhill veering slightly right up some steps as it avoids **Ebrington Hill Farm**. Keep going downhill into **Ebrington** and turn right onto the road.

3 **[SP 183404]** After about 75 metres take the footpath on the right up along the right-hand edge of a field and then diagonally up to the left in another field towards a road. Cross over the road and follow the footpath through several more fields before emerging onto a road. Turn right

60

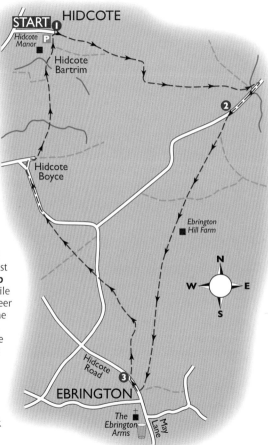

and at the T-junction take the left-hand fork towards **Hidcote Boyce** which will be reached after about 250 metres. Turn right (eastwards) past **Crabtree Cottage** and then up to a footpath fingerpost past a sign for **Top Farm**. At a stile into a field veer away from the hedge to the right and take the northerly path back towards **Hidcote Bartrim** and the National Trust car park at **Hidcote**.

winter

Cutsdean Village

20 Cutsdean
Changing times

4½ miles (7.2 km)

WALK HIGHLIGHTS

The walk starts high, then drops down into the valley, before a steep rise back up into wide-open spaces. Skylarks can be heard even in late February, adding to the pleasure of this winter walk. Despite some exposed stretches, the ground is relatively mud free, and the valleys and woods provide a degree of protection from the elements. Cutsdean was once a detached part of Worcestershire, owned by Worcester Abbey and standing in the Gloucestershire countryside as an isolated 'island'. In the early 20th century it became part of the parish

STARTING POINT & PARKING: Lay-by. From the B4077 travelling towards Stow-on-the-Wold, about a mile after the hamlet of Ford, turn left at a crossroads (signposted Snowshill and Broadway). Follow this past 'Jackdaws Castle'. After another 200 metres there is a crossroads, turn right and immediately there is a small lay-by on the left-hand side. **Sat Nav:** GL54 5XU.

MAP: OS Explorer OL 45 The Cotswolds. **Grid Ref:** SP 104308. **what3words:** bitters.polar.noisy

TERRAIN: Quiet country lanes and tracks. Footpaths and some field walking with some moderate gradients.

FOOD & DRINK: The Plough Inn, Ford, Temple Guiting, Cheltenham, GL54 5RU. ☎ 01386 584215. This is a popular pub with an open fireplace inside in the dining area, and a large beer garden with children's play area. The menu has plenty of pub classics as well as baguettes on offer.

of Temple Guiting, and officially part of the county of Gloucestershire. This beautiful and tranquil place still feels remote and separate from the outside world. Apart from some ruined barns, there are few, if any, buildings on this route. Part of the walk is along tures, identifiable by the ruins of moss-covered walls on either side. Tures were originally used to take animals to watering holes. The eagle-eyed will be able to spot the watering sites – the first is on the right where the route leaves the lane. The second is halfway along the valley bottom stretch between points 2 and 3 (look out for the pump workings added in the late 19th century).

THE WALK

[SP 104308] From the parking place, turn east (left with your back to the car) and walk down the lane. When the lane sweeps around to the left, keep straight on following the marked path. After passing through the gate walk uphill.

[SP 117305] At the brow of the hill turn to the left at a footpath sign towards the **Cutsdean Lodge** buildings. Follow the path downwards

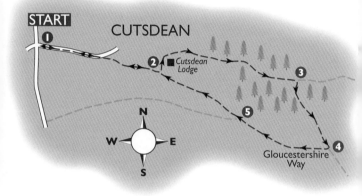

and over the stile to enter the wooded area. Follow the path along the valley bottom for about 1¼ miles.

③ **[SP 133305]** Just after a gate take the signed footpath to the right and follow this uphill through a wooded area to a wide path with a wall to the left. Go straight on with a field to the right.

④ **[SP 136298]** At the entrance to another wooded area, turn right onto a bridleway (**Gloucestershire Way**). Follow this into a field with the hedge to the right. After about 500 metres turn right through a gap in the hedge at a footpath sign and follow the path diagonally across some fields.

⑤ **[SP 126301]** At a copse leave the **Gloucestershire Way** by taking the right-hand signposted footpath through the copse and into a field. Follow this path back to the parking place,